BACK TO BASICS

TEN SESSION OUTLINES
FOR CHILDREN

NICK HARDING

First published in 1999 by
KEVIN MAYHEW LTD
Buxhall
Stowmarket
Suffolk IP14 3DJ

0 1 2 3 4 5 6 7 8 9

ISBN 1 84003 325 8
Catalogue No. 1500250

Cover design by Jonathan Stroulger
Illustrations by Simon Smith
Edited by Helen Elliot
Typesetting by Louise Selfe
Printed in Great Britain

Contents

	About the author	4
	Introduction	5
Session 1	Who is God?	9
Session 2	God the Father	15
Session 3	God the Son	21
Session 4	God the Spirit	27
Session 5	Man and God	33
Session 6	Obeying God	39
Session 7	Turning to God	45
Session 8	Belonging to God	51
Session 9	Following God	55
Session 10	God in the future	59

About the author

Nick Harding grew up in Birmingham, found faith at a Baptist Church, spent student days in Devon, taught for a few years near Nottingham, and has been up to his eyes in children's and youth work ever since! He lives near Sherwood Forest with his wife and two energetic sons, loves the music of Elton John and Elgar, supports Aston Villa, is a member of the Mother's Union, and travels on buses as a hobby! He works for his local cathedral, Southwell Minster, as Schools Officer where he also runs an award-winning educational project called 'Time Travelling!' He loves preaching, which he does every Sunday at churches of most denominations and traditions. Best recent moment – being really busy with a new challenge. Worst recent moment – fluffing the first line of a 'thought for the day' on BBC local radio!

Introduction

- Have you ever been stuck for material, and found that the time you put aside to plan has vanished?
- Have you ever struggled to use published material because it assumes the children have good Bible knowledge?

These are problems faced by everyone who works with children, whether in church or school. These session outlines are designed to meet your needs, with easy-to-prepare and varied material, including plenty of activity and lots for children to think about. They are aimed at children on the fringe of the church and those outside – perhaps who come to a holiday club, attend a midweek group, or go to the Christian group at school. They are intended for the 7-12 age group, but are adaptable for use with both younger and older groups. All the material here has been tried and tested over a number of years, and should provide all you need to help young people with no church experience get to grips with the nature of the Christian faith and ultimately God's love for them.

Each outline follows the same pattern, giving a number of sections which can be used. Remember that there is probably too much for one session, and you may want to miss items out or do them the following time. Other suggestions may be unsuitable for your group or facilities.

Theme

At the start of each outline is a clearly defined theme. This is to help you understand the point that the games, stories and talk suggestions are working towards.

Active game

There is at least one active game suggestion during each outline. This is provided to enable the young people to let off steam in a fun way, with a connection to the theme of the session.

Game

There is often another game which involves some of the group. Be aware that when asking for 'volunteers' you need to aim for a balance of boys and girls, able and less able, and so on.

Illustration

There are simple illustrations for a leader to act out included in some of these outlines. They introduce the theme of the session.

Quiz

Many of the outlines have a quiz suggestion to enable you to reinforce the point, or to introduce the theme. These are not meant to be too competitive, and shouldn't be taken too seriously!

Discussion

A vital skill to learn is the ability to express a point of view in a supportive environment. Discussion suggestions are provided to help you explore the theme and develop the children's skills in giving and receiving information.

Talk

Rather than having a discussion it is sometimes necessary for you to be clear about what you want to say. Some outlines include talks, with the main points listed.

Craft

These outlines include a craft suggestion where suitable and relevant. Most children learn best by doing, so it's good to include as much activity as possible in your plans. The craft suggestions require a minimum of equipment and resources.

Bible input

Every outline includes a Bible reference and a suggestion as to how you may want to tell the story. Remember that the children may be unfamiliar with the Bible, and it should always be presented in a positive and lively manner.

Prayer

At the end of each outline is a prayer or a prayer suggestion. These vary from being a quiet time for thought and meditation to being lively, aimed at children who are not used to praying and who may be embarrassed by it.

Memory chant

Each outline includes a simple chant on the theme of that day. These could be learned, memorised, repeated each session and added to as you go along, giving all the group members some basic truths to remember.

Songs

There are suggested songs given, but don't be restricted by this list. Most of them can be found in a large number of books and publishers including

ICC *Spring Harvest Big Book of Kids' Praise*

ICC *Kids' Praise 1995/1996/1997/1998*

ICC/Scripture Union *Everybody Praise*

HarperCollins *Junior Praise*

Kevin Mayhew *Children's Hymn Book, The Source*

SU Missions Dept. *J Team Songs*

BBC *Come and Praise, Books 1 and 2*

You may know and use much more relevant and suitable songs!

Funsheet

This is for you to photocopy and use either as part of the session or to give the children to take home and complete. It complements the session but does not have to be used at the same time. Ingredients include wordsearches, questions, puzzles, prayers, thought starters and quizzes.

You need to add . . .

(a) time for registration, notices, chatting, tuck shop, and whatever else is a normal part of your regular meetings

(b) your own wisdom, energy and creativity to make these outlines work for you and your young people

Other suggestions

• Use these outlines for a holiday club, decorating the room with 'B2B' and using it on the publicity posters and leaflets.

• Use the chant 'Back to Basics – back to God!' to a regular clapping rhythm. This helps reinforce the teaching message for the 10 sessions.

• If you have limited time each week split each of the sessions into two, providing a balance of activity and quiet in each.

• Try saying 'Amen' in different ways – shouting, winding up (ameeeeeeeeen), 'I agree' or 'Hey, that's cool!'

I hope *B2B: Back to Basics* helps you do your job with children more effectively, and I hope that through it more young people will come to know the life and love of Jesus for themselves.

With special thanks to
Alan Darlington and Clare

For all children's workers who care
about those outside the church.

Session 1   Who is God? _____

Theme   It is hard to define who God is, but we need to understand that he is all powerful and has real love for us.

Active game   *God is . . .*
Write the alphabet down a long sheet of paper or roll of wallpaper. Give each child a pen in turn, and they must think of one word that may describe God and write it next to the letter it begins with. Remember that it will get harder once you move towards Q, V, X and Z, and you are looking for the children's thoughts, so there are no right or wrong answers at this stage.

Game and talk   *Hangman*
Play *hangman* with the children in two teams, guessing the letters to fill in the gaps. After each word there is a Bible passage – if you feel it is appropriate read the passage out and explain what it says about who God is.

- Powerful: Psalm 29:4.
  God is very powerful. He made the world, everything in it, and us too! He is in control of the weather, the mountains and seas – he is in control of everything!

- Greatness: Psalm 145:3.
  God is the greatest, yet often we use his name wrongly, and swear instead of talking to him. Should we?

- Timeless: Psalm 89:2.
  God has lived for ever and will live for ever. He must have seen many millions of children grow up, yet he still knows us and loves us.

- Creator: Psalm 24:1-2.
  God made the whole world, and at first it was perfect as he had designed it. What is the world like now?

- Loving: Psalm 25:10.
  The great and mighty God who made everything loves us and cares about us. He wants us to love him too.

Bible input   Exodus 14; 15:22f; 16:1-16

God provides for Moses and the people

This story would be best told by a leader in their own words or read from a story Bible, the version in the Bible being a little long. Here are the main points to cover:

- The people of Israel were special to God, and he didn't want them to be slaves in Egypt.
- They had escaped, but then the King of Egypt had changed his mind and sent his army to catch them.
- They reached the Red Sea and couldn't escape. Moses prayed, and God held back the water for them all to cross in safety. The army behind them was destroyed.
- On the other side they were thirsty, but the only water they found tasted foul. God changed the water so they could drink it, and provided springs of fresh water for them the next day.
- The people became hungry. God sent down some manna, which was like bread. It landed on the ground along with small birds called quails. The people then had plenty to eat.

At the end of the story remind the children that although God was strong enough to hold back the water in the sea so the people could cross, he cared for their individual needs for food and water too. That shows us a little of what God is like.

Illustration

Ask one of the children to draw a triangle on a blackboard or sheet of paper. Explain that the triangle represents God – it is complete.

Rub out or cover up one side – the triangle is not a triangle any more.

There are three parts to God – the Father, the Son and the Holy Spirit. God has to be made up of all three, otherwise he is incomplete.

If possible have a boiling kettle, some cold water and some ice available. Explain that God is made up of three things which are all God but do different things. In the same way water, ice and steam are all made of water but they also do different things.

Craft

You will need:
- card
- scissors
- staplers
- pens and pencils

Ask each child to cut out three strips of card at least 20 cm long, and staple them together at the corners to form a triangle. Then write one of the following on each of the three sides:

God the Father – he made us
God the Son – he died for us
God the Spirit – he helps us

Memory chant   Learn this one this time:

God is one and God is three.
He made, he loved, and he helps me.

Prayer   Ask the children to repeat each line of this prayer after you have said it:

God, you are so powerful and strong
God, you are so loving and caring
God, you are so big and yet so near
God, thank you that you are here

Songs   Have you seen the pussycat?
My God is so big
He's got the whole world
Glorify your name
For God so loved . . .

1. Who is God?

B2B

Find 5 words that describe God.

greatpowerfulgodbiggreatnessjsptimewiselovingmcreatord

God Provides...

fill in the boxes with pictures (Exodus 14-16)

God holds back the sea.

God provides food.

God provides water.

How do you imagine God?

Chant

God is one and God is three —
He made, He loves and He helps me!

Session 2   God the Father _____

Theme   God the Father made the world and made us. Despite his power he still cares for everyone.

Active game   *The king*
Divide the children into groups of three. Give each group three cards folded so that the words cannot be seen. They should have the following characters written on them: King, Adviser and Villager. In addition the King cards should have a characteristic, such as 'Sad King/Generous King/Moody King/Happy King/Frightened King'. The children each choose a card and look at it. Then give them all five minutes to prepare a scene in which the Villager asks for something from the King, and the Adviser gives the King advice. Each group should then act out their scene to the others, who try to guess what the King is like.

Craft   You will need:
- paper
- pens and pencils

Talk for a short while about what makes a king, then ask each child to design and draw a poster with the top five rules they would put in place if they were king. When they have finished, talk about each rule and make a display of them if possible.

Game   *Fathers*
Ask for two children to volunteer. Each one should say a word that describes a good father, then the other says another word, and so on. There should be no repetition and no hesitation for longer than a couple of seconds. Please be aware and sensitive to the different situations in the group regarding fathers.

At the end of the game explain that God is the best father there could be. He is strong and loving, and he always wants the best for us, his children.

Bible input   2 Samuel 5:17-20; 19:24-30

David – powerful and caring

Ask the children to tell you everything they know about David.

15

Then read the following brief account of David's life. You may want to ask a child to act it out as you tell it.

David was the youngest in his family. His older brothers didn't really take much notice of him. They used to tease him for being smaller than them, and give him all the nasty jobs to do around the farm. David wasn't very old when he had to go out night and day to look after some of the sheep on the hillsides overlooking their house. It was a boring job, but David did it well and cared for the sheep, finding the best grass for them to eat and looking for any sheep that got lost. On one occasion he even killed a lion that was looking to attack the sheep.

One of David's other jobs was to see how his brothers were getting on and take them food. There was a big battle going on, and his brothers, with the rest of the army, were wondering how they could possibly fight the giant on the enemy side, Goliath. David decided that with God on his side he could kill the giant. Without any armour he stood firm and faced Goliath, who laughed at him. David used his sling to deadly effect again and struck Goliath hard on the head with a sharp stone so he collapsed and died.

Despite David winning the battle, and playing the harp for the King, King Saul still hated him and tried to kill him. It was many years of hiding and hard work before David became King. He fought many battles, won many wars, and escaped many attacks. But even at the end of all his hard work he still cared for people. One day King Saul's grandson, Mephibosheth, came to King David expecting to be put to death. Instead King David was kind to him and offered him riches. David was a brave boy, a strong and fearless young man, and a good and caring King.

Game

David says . . .
Play 'David says . . .' in the same way as you would play 'Simon says . . .' Give instructions which the children should follow as long as they are prefaced with 'David says . . .'; if not then the children who get it wrong are out.

Talk

David was powerful, yet even he was not as strong, powerful or caring as his and our Father God. God is stronger than any of us, and if we want help in anything he has the power to help us. David realised this and wrote many songs and psalms to God the Father.

Memory chant

Learn this chant this session:

David was a really great King;
but Father God's better than anything.

Prayer   Copy out part of one of David's songs to God, Psalm 103:1-3, 12-13, 19-22. Then read it together as a group.

Songs   He's got the whole world
God loves you, he cares about you
My God is so big
God is our Father
Your ways are higher than mine

Session 3   God the Son

Theme

God the Son is Jesus, who came to earth and grew as a child. He lived, suffered and died to bring us closer to God.

Game

Jesus is . . .

Ask two or three children to come out and for each to speak for 15 seconds, telling the others all they know about Jesus. If they do not manage to keep talking they are out and the next child has a go.

Active game

Speaker and doer

Put two large sheets of paper on the wall at opposite ends of the room. Then talk to the children, asking them what they know about what Jesus did. Most of the recorded events in the Gospels indicate that Jesus was a speaker (speaking, teaching, telling) and a doer (healing, walking, miracles). Remind the children of a number of miracles and sayings of Jesus, and then ask them to run from one end of the room to the other, writing up relevant things about Jesus the Son at each end.

Illustration

Have an illustrated copy of the Good News Bible available, or copy some of the line pictures from the gospels in this version. Show the children some of the pictures, one at a time, and explain what is happening in each one. Point out what happened, who else was there, what the people were doing, when in Jesus' life it happened, and so on.

Bible input

Mark 10:46-52

Blind Bartimaeus

Deliver this story in your own words, preferably with two leaders acting it out as a drama sketch rather than telling it. Make sure that the following points are made clearly:

- Jesus was, as usual, surrounded by a noisy and needy crowd.

- Bartimaeus shouted, but the others in the crowd wanted him to be quiet.

- Despite the noise, Jesus heard him and went to help.

- Bartimaeus really knew that Jesus was special and could help him. He had real faith.

Talk Recap on the story, pointing out that Jesus really cared for Bartimaeus and paid attention to him despite the crowd around them both. God sent his Son to help us all in the same way, so that he could show his love for us. The things Jesus did, like the healings, teachings and his painful death, were to show how much he loves each of us. Jesus treated Bartimaeus as an individual, and that's how he treats us, too.

Quiz Write up the following sayings of Jesus with the underlined words missed out. Nearby display another sheet of paper with a list of the missing words in the wrong order. The children should be split into two teams and try to match up the words with the sayings so that each one makes sense. After each one is worked out, explain briefly what it means and what it says about Jesus.

To make the game more interesting and challenging you could include some wrong and inappropriate words on the word list.

1. I am the <u>light</u> of the world.
2. I am <u>with</u> you always.
3. I have come to <u>give</u> you life in <u>all</u> its fullness.
4. I am the <u>vine</u> and you are the <u>branches</u>.
5. Love <u>one another</u> as I have <u>loved</u> you.
6. Go into all the <u>world</u>.
7. You are like <u>salt</u> for all <u>mankind</u>.
8. I am the bread of <u>life</u>.

Craft You will need:
- paper
- pens and pencils

Remind the children of some of the things Jesus did in his life, and ask them to draw a cartoon story of Jesus doing one or two of the miracles mentioned. This could be a competition with someone else judging which one is the best.

Memory chant This is the next one to learn:

Jesus came for you and me,
and he loves us personally.

Prayer Provide each child with a stone. If possible go outside and ask the children each to find and pick up one stone.

Sit in a circle and look at the stones, explaining that each one is different and yet they are all stones. Remind the children that we are all different, yet Jesus loves us and cares about us individually. He knows what we are like and wants to help us with the things we don't like.

Finish a time of quiet by saying this short prayer:

Thank you, Jesus,
that you know me and you love me. Amen

Songs
Jesus, Jesus
Jesus is greater than the greatest heroes
Jesus' love is a powerful love
Jesus' love is very wonderful
Jesus, name above all names
God knows me

B2B 3. God the Son.

Chant

Jesus came for you and me, and he loves us personally.

JESUS SAID...

Connect the words with the pictures.

I am the Light of the World.

I am the Bread of Life.

I am the Vine.

Go into all the World.

Finish this prayer:
alive, died

Thank you Jesus, that you _____ for me. Thank you that you are _____ now. Amen.

Blind Bartimaeus

find 10 words from the story (Mark 10:46-52)

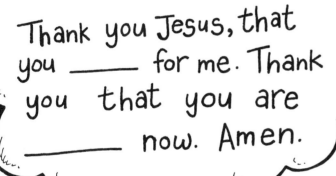

W	E	L	L	B	L	I	N	J	C
F	B	E	G	G	A	R	Z	E	R
A	L	A	R	G	E	O	W	S	O
P	I	T	Y	V	M	A	N	U	W
U	N	J	E	S	X	D	K	S	D
Q	D	R	O	A	F	A	I	T	H

Road   Pity
well   Jesus
man   blind
Beggar faith
large
        crowd

Session 4   God the Spirit _____

Theme

God the Spirit is the helper Jesus promised to his disciples. The Spirit can make a difference in our lives.

Active game

Piggyback relay race
This is probably best done outside on some grass to avoid accidents, and needs to be well controlled!

Split the children into two teams and line them up in pairs. The front pair have to race, with one on the back of the other, to the far end of the room and back without the rider falling off. Then the next pair race, and so on until all the children have taken part in the race. The winning team is the one that gets all the team to the end and back first.

Illustration

Ask two children to come out to the front and take part in a short demonstration. Ask them to sit on the floor back-to-back and then link their arms. They should now stand up by pushing against each other without going on to their knees or using their hands. If the first pair is not successful then choose another pair to give it a try.

Once you have finished, explain to the children how that illustration and the previous game relied on people working together. You can't have a piggyback if no one will carry you, and you can't stand up as a linked pair unless you both push at the same time.

Discussion and talk

Talk about any times when the children have got lost. Perhaps you can remember an incident to tell them about from your own childhood. Explore some of the feelings involved in being lost, including loneliness, sorrow, fear, panic, and so on.

The disciples felt lost when Jesus went up to heaven. They had just got used to the fact that he had beaten death and come alive again, and now they felt alone once more. They knew that a large number of people had not liked Jesus, and would pick on them, his followers.

Some of the disciples had remembered that Jesus had promised to send help for them after he had gone up to heaven: 'I will ask the Father and he will send another helper, who will stay with you for ever' (John 14:15).

They met together to pray and talk regularly, but they didn't really know what this 'helper' would do — what did it mean?

Bible input
Acts 2:1-13

The Holy Spirit comes

Split the children into three groups, giving each group one of the following phrases to learn:

They must be drunk!

What's happening?

This is great!

Then tell the story of the first Pentecost, pointing to the relevant group when you want them to say their line. Cover the following points:

- The disciples were all gathered in an upstairs room, ready to pray and sing together.

- They had no idea that the promised helper, the Holy Spirit, was going to come then.

- They heard a sound like a rushing wind and saw what looked like flames settling on each other's heads.

- At once they began to speak in languages which they did not actually know!

- There was a large crowd of people from different countries gathered, and they were amazed to hear these local men speaking their own home languages.

- The disciples were amazed, and were enjoying the Holy Spirit.

- Some in the crowd thought that the disciples must be drunk – it was too unbelievable to be really happening.

- The Holy Spirit stayed with them and helped them from then on.

Craft
You will need:
- bright paper
- scissors

Ask all the children to cut out of bright paper a quantity of flame shapes of varying sizes, and put all the flames in a bag. These will be used in the quiz that follows.

Quiz
Have the bag of flames available. Then split the children into two teams and ask them questions. The child who answers correctly can choose a flame from the bag without looking. At the end of the quiz the team with the biggest flame is the winner.

Q. What was the helper called?
A. *The Holy Spirit*

Q. Where was the room?
A. *Upstairs/Jerusalem*

Q. Why had the disciples got together?
A. *Pray/talk*

Q. What happened after the sound of a wind?
A. *Tongues of flame*

Q. What new ability had the disciples got?
A. *Speak in other languages*

Q. How did the crowd react?
A. *Amazed*

Q. What did some people think the disciples had been doing?
A. *Drinking*

Q. How long was the Holy Spirit with them?
A. *For ever*

Memory chant

Learn this one this time:

The Holy Spirit helps us know
all we need to help us grow.

Prayer

Teach the children the following response:

'Thank you, God, that you are with me now.'

You were there with the disciples when they needed help.
Thank you . . .
You were there with the crowd when they needed to hear.
Thank you . . .
You are with me and help me learn more about you.
Thank you . . .

Songs

Spirit of the living God
God is so good
Be bold, be strong
Lord, you put a tongue in my mouth

THE HOLY SPIRIT COMES

DRAW THE SCENE HERE

THESE PEOPLE HELP ME

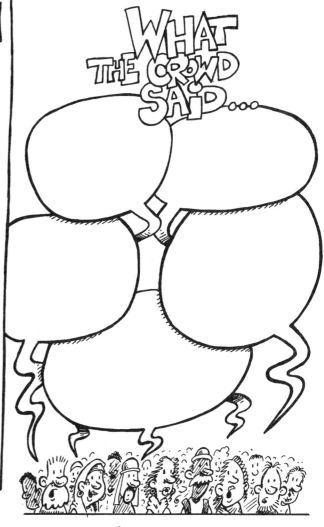

WHAT THE CROWD SAID...

Chant

The Holy Spirit helps us know,

all we need to help us grow!

Session 5   Man and God _____

Theme

God made us all, and he loves us. God cares for all mankind, whatever we do and however we treat him.

Active game

Animals
Give all the children a piece of paper with the name of one of the six animals listed on it. Then give them two minutes to get into groups of the same animal by making noises that the particular animal makes.

Cow, Cat, Dog, Lion, Sheep, Chicken

Game

Mirrors
Ask all the children to sit facing each other, and number themselves 1 and 2 in each pair. Child 1 has to act out what they do from getting up to going to school each day, while child 2 has to copy the actions as if they were a mirror. Then child 2 acts out all that they do from going home from school until bedtime, while child 1 has to mirror every action.

Illustration

Ask each child to look very carefully at the person they are sitting next to. No one will have seen someone the same as them. People are all different, as different as all the animals are. Yet God made us, and we are all part of his creation.

Quiz

Have a large number of balloons blown up and ready. Split the children into two teams and bring one child from each group out to the front. Then ask them these questions, and each time a team gets an answer correct the child at the front gets given a balloon to hold. The winning team is the one with the most balloons. These questions will reveal a little of the group's Bible knowledge, and they may need clues to get the right answer.

Q. Who was the first woman God made?
A. *Eve*

Q. Who was the first man God made?
A. *Adam*

Q. What did they do wrong?
A. *Ate the fruit*

Q. Who built a boat in the desert?
A. *Noah*

33

Q. Why did he do it?
A. *Because God told him to*

Q. Why did God send a flood?
A. *To clean the world*

Q. How did God come to earth?
A. *As Jesus*

Q. Why did he send Jesus?
A. *To show how much he loves us*

Q Did the people care for Jesus?
A. *No*

Q. What did they do to him?
A. *Killed him*

Q What was the 'helper' called?
A. *The Holy Spirit*

Q What did the disciples see on their heads?
A. *Flames*

Bible input

The perfect world is spoiled
Read out the following passages or put them in your own words. Get children to act out some of the parts.

Adam and Eve
God made a wonderful world, which was perfect. On the last of the seven days of creation he sat back, looked at it and decided that it was really good. But God had also made a man and a woman, and it was not long before things started to go wrong. There was a tree which God had told them not to touch, but they did anyway. They ate the fruit and immediately realised that they had done wrong. Full of guilt, they tried to hide from God, but he knew that they had done wrong and spoiled the perfect world he had made.

The flood
Things went from bad to worse, and the children of Adam and Eve did evil things. God looked at the world he had made and saw only a few people who listened to him – a man called Noah and his family. He decided it was time to clean the world up, so he told Noah to build a big boat for himself, his family and two of every kind of animal. When the flood came the boat floated on the water for many days, and the world was clean again. But things still went wrong.

The Messiah
The people of God still failed to do what God wanted them to. They would often ignore him and tell lies. In the end God promised them a saviour, the Messiah, who would come and

34

help those who would listen to him. The Messiah was God's own son, Jesus. A few people listened to Jesus but most turned against him, and he was killed by being nailed to a wooden cross. But Jesus was not beaten, and two days later he came alive again.

Talk

God made the world perfect and gave it to mankind, yet it all went wrong. We still let God down every time we hurt someone, or swear or insult others or steal. Many years ago people used to kill animals to say 'sorry' to God. Jesus died to stop us having to kill animals – we can now say 'sorry' and be forgiven by God.

Craft

You will need:

- card
- scissors
- pens and pencils
- string

Ask each child to cut out two circles at least 15 cm in diameter. Then cut each one from one edge to the centre. The circles should then be coloured in on both sides as if they are the world, and slotted together through the slits. Add string to make this an attractive mobile.

World mobile

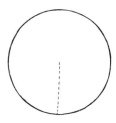  

Memory chant

Learn this chant this time:

We made a mess of God's great plan;
we should love him all we can.

Prayer

Remind the children that God made us all, and he knows us really well. Then ask them to be quiet as you read out Psalm 139:1-6, 13-17.

Songs

Thank you, Jesus
God's way
Step by step
I reach up high

5. Man and God.

Man AND God

Dear God,
I am sorry for
the things I do wrong
like _____, _____
and _____. Thank
you that you
forgive me. Amen.

Adam and Eve eat
the fruit.

Jesus
dies on
a cross.

Nothing.

God makes
the world.

The Holy
Spirit
comes.

Noah's boat.

Jesus is
born.

Put a line ⤳ between the
pictures in the right order.

WRONG X THINGS

Write here the wrong
things people do.

Chant

We made a
mess of God's
great plan -
we should love
Him all
we can!

Session 6   Obeying God _____

Theme   There are many people we have to obey, but it is always best to obey God and do what he wants us to.

Active game   *Beans*
Make sure that each of the children is in some space. Then call out the following types of beans in quick succession and in varied orders. The children should get into the shape suggested by the type of bean as described:

Runner beans – *running on the spot*

Kidney beans – *bent kidney-shape with the body*

Broad beans – *standing or lying as wide as possible*

Stringy beans – *hands up and down as if pulling lengths of string*

Has-beans (!) – *bent over, walking-stick mime*

Quiz   Split the children into teams with 4-6 in each. Give each of the teams cards with the following letters: A, C, D, D, E, E, H, I, L, N, N, O, O, P, R, S, T, Y. Read out the following clues one by one. The teams must spell out the answers using the cards and then stand up holding them in the correct order. Write up the answers on a sheet of paper:

Q. Who works at your school and teaches you things?
A. *Teacher*

Q. Who tells you what medicine to take?
A. *Doctor*

Q. Who looks after you at home?
A. *Parents*

Q. Who wear uniforms and try to stop crime?
A. *Police*

Q. Who looks after food and children at school lunchtime?
A. *Dinner lady*

Talk   We have already learned a lot about instructions. We followed the instructions so that we could play the beans game correctly. We have discovered that there are people who we should listen to and obey. If we don't follow the instructions we are given it can end badly – we may get hurt, end up in trouble, or upset others. It is always best to follow and obey the instructions we get.

Bible input

2 Kings 5:1-14

Naaman is healed

Tell the story direct from the Bible or act it out with two people as given here. Play it in a chatty and light style.

A.   So, you were saying – you are a servant of Naaman?

B.   Yes. My master is the commander of the Syrian army and very powerful.

A.   But hadn't he got an awful skin disease?

B.   He had, but now he hasn't! It was an amazing time when he got healed, I can tell you.

A.   So, why don't you tell me?

B.   Right, I will. Naaman had been suffering with the nasty skin disease for a long time, and really wanted to get rid of it. He took medicines and put cream on, but it didn't seem to want to go. Then he heard about the God of Israel and one of his messengers called Elisha, so we all set off to find Elisha. When we got to where he was staying Elisha had the cheek only to send a servant out, and not appear to see Naaman himself. What's more, the message was that Naaman should wash in the River Jordan seven times and he would get better. Naaman thought it was a cruel joke and was really cross.

A.   So did Naaman leave?

B.   Well, no, he didn't. Elisha sent another message telling Naaman to wash seven times in the river, and Naaman decided it was worth a try. So he obeyed the old man and washed.

A.   And then . . .

B.   Then he was better! His skin was pure and strong, with no mark of the disease. Naaman was overjoyed, and went running to Elisha saying, 'Now I know that the God of Israel is the only true God.'

A.   I wonder what would have happened if Naaman hadn't obeyed Elisha.

B.   I've got no doubt – he would not have been healed!

Craft

You will need:

• card

• pens and pencils

Give each child a piece of card and ask them to fold it so it stands on its own. On the front they should write, 'I obey

God's instructions', and on the inside draw all the ways God gives us instructions. These could include through the Bible, through leaders, through prayer, through friends, and so on.

Discussion

Lead the children in their thinking about the story of Naaman by asking the following questions:

- How did Elisha know what to tell Naaman to do? God told him.

- Why did Naaman not want to wash himself seven times? He thought it was silly.

- What did Naaman have to learn to do? Obey.

Remind the children that it is always best to obey those who try to help us, and God wants to help us all. If we need to know what to do we should obey God.

Memory chant

Learn this chant this session:

God knows what to do and say.
It's got to be best to think and obey.

Prayer

Pray this prayer on behalf of the whole group:

God, we thank you
    that you know what is best for us.
Help us to hear you,
    help us to listen to you,
    and help us to obey you. Amen

Songs

Safe in the Father's hands
With Jesus in the boat
Your ways are higher than mine
God has got a plan
Live my life by faith

Session 7   Turning to God _____

Theme   God made us and knows us. The best decision we can make in life is to decide to turn to him and follow him.

Game   *Ding dong*
Stand all the children in a circle. A ball is passed from one to another following the instructions for 'ding' and 'dong' given below. When the children have caught on to the idea, speed it up, and then add 'dang' and 'dung'!

Ding   *Pass the ball clockwise*
Dong   *Pass the ball anti-clockwise*
Dang   *Throw the ball across the circle to another child*
Dung   *Turn round and throw the ball backwards over your head*

Discussion   Talk about the journeys that the children go on. Ask these questions:

- Why do they go on journeys?
- Who are they going to see?
- What do they do on the journey?
- What do they expect to happen on the journey?
- Do unexpected things sometimes happen on the journey?

Mention that life is often described as a journey, and there are many things that happen to us on our journey through life that are unplanned and unexpected.

Craft   You will need:

- A3 paper
- pens and pencils

Give each child a strip of paper half the width of a sheet of A3 paper. Explain that they should put their own journey of life from birth to now on one side, including events such as birth, first birthday, accidents, nursery, starting school, moving house, and so on. On the other side they should draw the way they would like their journey of life to go on from here, including school and exams, job, home, family, and so on.

Bible input   Acts 8:26-40

Philip and the Ethiopian official

Read the full account of what happened in the story from a

suitable version of the Bible, encouraging the children to listen carefully. You may want to get two children to act out the story as you tell it.

Quiz

Spot the difference
Read the same Bible passage (Acts 8:26-40) again, this time putting in some deliberate mistakes that stop the passage making sense. The child who spots a mistake should stand up and tell you what they think the correct word should be. Example: As he *sailed* along he was reading from the book of *Thomas the Tank Engine*.

Talk

The Ethiopian was reading parts of the Bible that he did not have any chance of understanding. He knew it was good to read, but he didn't know what it meant. When Philip joined him he was able to explain the meaning of the words, and it meant so much to the Ethiopian that he stopped where he was and changed his life. He found out that Jesus had died for him and loved him.

Active game

Place parts of the following code on cards around the room:

A B D E F G I J L O R S T U V W Y
! " £ $ % & * ( ) - + = # ? @ < >

Give each of the children one of the following messages written out on a piece of paper without the decoding letters. If you think this may be too difficult, let the children work in pairs or threes.

& - £   ) - @ $ =   > - ?

God loves you

& - £ =   < ! >   * =   " $ = #

God's way is best

($ = ? =   £ * $ £   % - +   ? =

Jesus died for us

After all the messages have been decoded, sit down and talk through what each of them means.

Memory chant   This is the one for this session:

God goes with us every day,
I'll turn to him – he knows the way.

Prayer   Play some quiet music in the background while you read out again Acts 8:34-38. Ask the children to think about how God loves them and wants them to turn to him.

Songs   So I've made up my mind
Step by step
Here I am
Father God, I wonder
One more step along the world I go
God goes with us

the JOURNEY

fill in what Philip and the Ethiopian say...

The Ethiopian (Acts 8) v 26-40)

Circle the words that are wrong:

Philip met the Ethiopian Woman on the train. The Ethiopian was reading from the Bible, but he couldn't sing what it meant. Philip travelled with him and explained all about the songs. The Ethiopian wanted to be loved by Jesus once he understood.

MY JOURNEYS

WHERE DO YOU GO?

WHO DO YOU SEE?

WHAT DO YOU DO ON YOUR JOURNEY?

chant

God goes with us every day – I'll turn to Him, He Knows the way!

Session 8 Belonging to God _____

Theme

Once we turn to God, he accepts us and invites us to follow him always. There is never any need to be alone again.

Active game

Belonging

The children should wander around the room until you shout out one of the following. When you do that they have to get into the groups you describe as quickly as possible.

- Groups of boys and groups of girls
- Groups of trainer-wearers and non trainer-wearers
- Groups of five
- Groups of three
- Groups of their ages
- Groups of birthday months

Group craft

You will need:

- scissors, glue, paper, pens

Split the children into smaller groups and ask them to list all of the things they can think of that are wrong – swearing, stealing, lies, and so on. Then they should cut out the individual words that were listed and stick them to another piece of paper in the shape of the word 'sin'. All of these things are wrong, and in order to belong to God we must ask him to forgive us and we must try not to do them again.

Story

Read this story, asking, 'What would you do?' at the appropriate points.

Miss Snodgrass was the least popular teacher in school. She seemed to shout all the time, and never let anyone get away with doing anything wrong. Everyone dreaded upsetting her – when she was angry she could get really mean and nasty!

It was during an ordinary lesson one morning when the headteacher came in. 'Miss Snodgrass, you must go to the telephone now – there is an urgent message for you. Leave the class; I am sure they will be fine for a couple of minutes.'

What would you do?

As Miss Snodgrass left the room she looked uneasy, and decided to get back there as quickly as she could just in case. Soon the children heard the last of her footsteps in the corridor.

What would you do?

Then most of them were out of their seats, swopping chairs, shouting and running about. Charlotte and a few others stayed in their places and tried to get on with their work, while one or two stood by the door keeping a lookout for Miss Snodgrass. 'She's coming', the cry went up . . .

What would you do?

. . . and in a flash they were all sitting down, appearing to work. In fact Miss Snodgrass wouldn't have thought anything had happened had it not been for the message on the blackboard: 'Miss Snodgrass is a grotbag.'

What would you do?

Her face went through a range of colours including purple, black and yellow before she turned to the class in a fury, demanding to know who had written it. No one dared own up, and they were kept in at breaktime.

What would you do?

At lunchtime she tried again, but there was still no explanation. Finally, when she asked again, Charlotte owned up. The class knew that Charlotte could not be to blame – she never did anything wrong.

What would you do?

Miss Snodgrass didn't know what to say, and gave Charlotte a punishment of tidying the classroom for a week. Charlotte had taken the blame on behalf of the whole class. In the same way Jesus died on the cross, taking the blame for all we have ever done wrong.

Illustration

If possible, bring in a baby doll and talk to the children about what it is like for a baby to have to learn new things all the time. Babies are fresh and new, and have a lot of growing to do. In the same way, God invites people to belong to him, and they become like babies, too. Jesus talked of people being 'born again', which means starting afresh as one of God's people.

Memory chant

Here's the one for this session:
It may be hard, it may seem odd,
but I want to belong to God!

Prayer

Give the children each a piece of paper and pencil, and allow them to write their own prayer to God. It can be read out to the others or remain private between the child and God.

Songs

I have decided to follow Jesus
Here I am
Your ways are higher
God's love will never end

Further information

Books and leaflets for children who are considering belonging to God are available from Christian bookshops.

B2B — 8. Belonging to God.

Miss Snodgrass said...

Miss Snodgrass was an angry teacher. What do you think she said?

JESUS

Fill in the gaps

us
cross
wrong
blame
died

Jesus
_ _ _ _ on
the _ _ _ _ _ for all of
_ _.
He took the
_ _ _ _ _
for all we do
_ _ _ _

I BELONG TO...

Circle the groups that you belong to, and write in any others:

- Cubs   football   School
  Church   Brownies
- Netball   family   music

Chant

It may be hard, it may seem odd, but I want to belong to God!

Session 9   Following God

Theme

The best future for us is to be found in God. We all need to go on with him now and for ever.

Active game

I like . . .

Sit all the children in a circle. One child begins 'I like . . .' and fills in the gap with something they like. The next child continues with '(s)he likes . . . and I like . . .', and so on until it gets back to the first child. Those near the end have a lot of things to remember.

Game

All about you

Ask the children to sit in pairs with people they would not normally sit with. Give them two minutes each to find out all there is to know about the other by asking questions.

Talk

We all know the people we live with really well. For many of us we will have lived with them most or all of our lives. We know how they feel, and we face the future together. We need to get to know each other because, if we are going to follow God, we have to live and work together as a family. The Bible helps us get to know more about God as we learn to live as a family of followers, and it shows us what we should be like as followers.

Craft activity

A good friend

You will need:

- large sheets of paper
- felt marker pens

Place two pieces of paper on the floor, one headed 'A good friend' and the other headed 'A bad friend'. Ask the children to talk about it among themselves and then go from one sheet to the other, writing in what they think a good friend and a bad friend should be like.

Bible input

Luke 10:30-37

The Good Samaritan

Read this story from the Bible or a story Bible, or tell it in your own words, covering the following key incidents. It is great fun to involve children as actors while you tell this story.

- The man was travelling alone when he was brutally attacked.
- The robbers left him with nothing, and he was badly injured.

- Two very religious men came along, but neither of them stopped to help. They both walked on the other side of the road to avoid him.

- A Samaritan came along. Samaritans were hated by most people.

- The Samaritan helped the injured traveller, took him to where he could recover, and paid the bill.

Game   *Follow the leader*
Play this traditional game around the room and outside, nominating different children to lead from time to time. Ask them to be as creative as they like in the actions they expect the others to do. For the game to work properly everyone must copy the leader and do as the leader does.

Talk   Think back to the story of the Good Samaritan, who was willing to help the helpless stranger. We are all like the traveller – we are nothing, injured by the world and suffering at the side of the road. In the same way that the hated Samaritan helped the injured man, so God helps us. He has picked us up, healed our wounds and invited us to travel with him from now on.

If we are to follow God always we must remember that we are like the man who was attacked. To help protect ourselves we need to learn more about God and get to grips with what he tells us to do in the Bible.

Memory chant   Here is the one to learn this time:

You pick me up, you see me through,
Father God, I'll follow you.

Prayer   Lead the children in this prayer, with this response:

'I will follow you.'

When things are going really well
I will . . .
When I am tired or ill
I will . . .
When I feel sad and hurt
I will . . .
Now I am young and when I am older
I will . . .

Songs   God is our Father
My God is so big
Live my life by faith
The journey of life

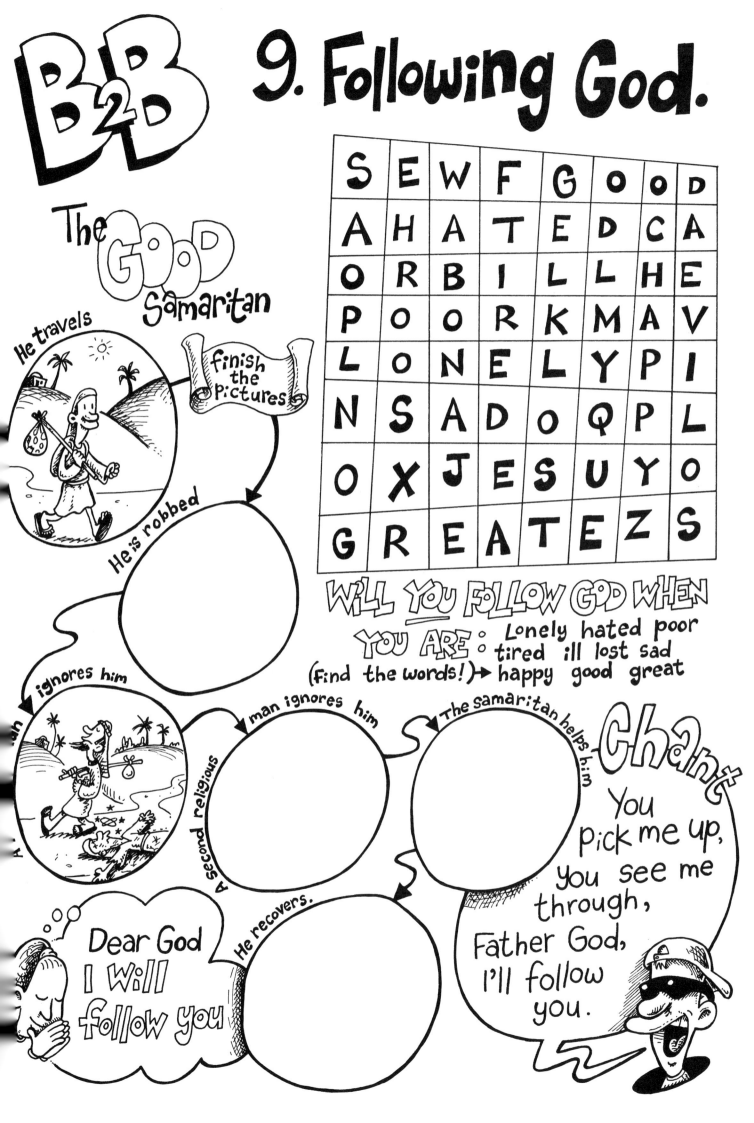

Session 10   God in the future _____

Theme

God was there at the beginning and will be there at the end. The future is his, and we can all be part of it.

Active game

Beginning and End
Explain to the children that one end of the room is the beginning and the other is the end. They must go to the correct place every time you say 'beginning' or 'end'. Then read this passage or make up your own:

God was there in the beginning. There was no end to the things he made. There was nothing at the beginning, but after a week he had made the world and all the things in it. At the end of the week of creation he decided that it had been a good beginning. But the end of the peace was to come, and people were beginning to damage the world that God had made. In the end God sent his own Son, beginning as a baby born in a stable, and at the end dying on the cross. But that was just the beginning of Christianity, for Jesus came alive again and went up to heaven to be with his and our Father God. The end is still to come, and, just like he was there in the beginning, God will be there at the end.

Quiz

Split the children into two groups and ask the following questions. Each child who answers correctly can stand at the front. The group with the most people standing at the front will be the winner.

Q. Who did David kill with a stone?
A. *Goliath*

Q. What was the name of the King who hated David?
A. *Saul*

Q. What did God help his people cross over?
A. *Red Sea*

Q. Who made Bartimaeus well?
A. *Jesus*

Q. What did the disciples hear when the Holy Spirit came?
A. *Wind*

Q. What did some of the crowd think had happened?
A. *They were drunk*

Q. What did Adam and Eve do that was wrong?
A. *Ate the fruit*

Q. Why did God send a flood?
A. *To clean the world*

Q. What was wrong with Naaman?
A. *Skin disease*

Q. Who did Philip go to help?
A. *The Ethiopian*

Q. Who in the Bible talked about being 'born again'?
A. *Jesus*

Q. How many religious men ignored the injured traveller?
A. *Two*

Bible input

Revelation 21:1-5

The end of time

Explain that only God knows what it will be like at the end of time, but the last book in the Bible, Revelation, is all about some of the things that might be seen. It has lots of interesting and complicated images, and it is very hard to understand.

Read out the passage, and then repeat the following points:

* At the end of time this world, with all its mess, will vanish away and be replaced by something new and better.

* All things will be new, clean and perfect. They will be the best gift mankind can have.

* God will live for ever with his people on the new earth.

* All nasty things like sorrow and pain will have vanished, and we will be left with all good things.

Discussion

Have two large pieces of paper available. Lead the children to think about all the good things that will be in the new earth, such as purity, no pollution, health, love, joy, and such-like. Then ask them to think about all the bad things that will have gone, like pain, hurt, sorrow, sin, murder, pollution, greed, and so on. Write up one list on one piece of paper, and the other list on the other piece of paper. Explain that no one knows when all this will happen, but God will only do what is best for all people, including us.

Game

Opposites
Ask a child to come out. As you say the following words, the child must respond with the opposite as quickly as they can. If they hesitate for too long another child can take over and have a go.

Hot (cold)   Fast (slow)

Solid (liquid)   Tall (short)
Fat (thin)   Wide (narrow)
Warm (cool)   Happy (sad)
Sick (well)   Better (worse)
Rich (poor)   Nice (nasty)

Memory chant   The final chant to learn:

God was the beginning, he is the end,
God is the best Father, he is the best friend.

Prayer   Give each child a sheet of paper with three equal columns. The columns should be headed 'Sorry', 'Thanks' and 'I will . . .' Ask the children to plan and write their own prayers individually, using the columns and thinking about each topic.

You may want to invite those who feel able to read their prayers to the others in a few minutes of quiet.

Songs   He's got the whole world
Your ways are higher than mine
My God is so big
God has got a plan
Who's the king of the jungle?

NEW WORLD

DRAW the NEW WORLD here

AT the END...

(Revelation 21:3)
Unravel the words and write them in...

I _____ (draeh) a loud

_____ (ciove) speaking

from _____ (het) throne:

Now _____ (sdoG),

home is with

_____ (nKimnad) .

_____

New World

Bad things X | Good things ✓

List BAD things that would go and Good things there would be in your NEW WORLD.

Chant

God was the beginning,
He is the end,
God is the best father,
He is the best friend.